TABLE OF CONTENTS

Pre-test 2
1 Simple Sentences 6
2 Interrogative Sentences 8
3 Inverted Sentences 10
4 Imperative Sentences 12
5 Compound Sentences 14
6 Complex Sentences 16
7 Parallel Structure 18
8 Misplaced Modifiers 20
9 Subject-Verb Agreement 22
10 Avoid Unnecessary Shifts in Tenses 24
11 Prepositional Phrases 26
12 Sentence Fragments Without Subject and Verb .28
13 Sentence Fragments Without Verbs 30
14 Run-on Sentences 32
15 Dangling Phrases 34
16 Avoid Wordiness 36
17 Commas 38
18 Capitalization 40
19 End Punctuation 42
Post Test 44

Reviewer

Sandra R. Evans
Teacher of English/Language Arts
ABC Unified School District
Lakewood, California

Editors: Monica Glina, Renée Beach, Stephanie Cahill, Phyllis Dunsay, Douglas Falk, Jennifer McCarthy
Editorial Assistants: Marilyn Bashoff, Patrice Moncrieff
Designers: Joan Jacobus, Evelyn Bauer, Jennifer Visco
Editorial Development: Pencil Point Studio
Production Editors: Suzanne Keezer, Mark Andreotti,

Copyright ©1999 by Globe Fearon, Inc., One Lake Street, Upper Saddle River, New Jersey, 07458, www.globefearon.com. All rights reserved. No part of this book may be reproduced or transmitted in any form or by any means, electronic, photographic, mechanical, or otherwise, including photocopying, recording, or by any information storage and retrieval system, without permission in writing from the publisher.

Printed in the United States of America
 3 4 5 6 7 8 9 10   04 03 02 01

ISBN 0-130-23256-4

MT. MADONNA HIGH SCHOOL
8750 Hirasaki Court
Gilroy, California 95020

1-800-848-9500
www.globefearon.com

Pre-test

The following pre-test will help you determine where you need further practice in *Sentences*. Take the test in one sitting, answering every question. If you need more practice on any topics, turn to the Exercises listed.

Read the sentences below. Write the simple subject and simple predicate.

For more practice, go to Exercise:

1. Melissa shops for groceries on Thursdays.

    The simple subject is: _____

    The simple predicate is: _____

    `1`

2. Are you leaving the theater?

    The simple subject is: _____

    The simple predicate is: _____

    `2`

Identify the following sentences as interrogative or imperative.

3. Have you listened to your new CD player? _____   `2`

4. Please leave immediately! _____   `4`

Read the inverted sentence. Write the simple subject and verb.

5. Will you join us for dinner tonight?

    Simple subject: _____

    Verb: _____

    `3`

Identify the understood subject in the sentence below.

6. Disregard that section of the training manual.

    The understood subject is: _____

    `4`

Join the following two simple sentences to create a compound sentence.

7. The police officers trained the dogs.
   The customs department used them for law enforcement.

Which word in the following sentence joins two compound sentences?

8. The car would not start, so we called a towing company. _____

Read the complex sentence below. Underline the dependent clause.

9. Until Sharon volunteered in a hospital, she had never considered nursing as a career choice.

Correct the following sentence by changing the words or phrases to the same form. Write the new sentence on the lines.

10. The painter opened the can, mixed the paint, and pouring some into a tray.

Underline the misplaced modifier in this sentence. Then, write the sentence correctly.

11. Clarissa gave the prepared research paper to her professor nervously.

Underline the verb in parentheses that agrees with the subject.

12. The supervisor (follows, follow) the regulations closely.

Underline the verb that shifts tense in the following passage.

13. Yesterday, Eton checked the office supply list. He ordered paper, pencils, and staples. Then he takes the last box of file labels in the supply cabinet.

For more practice, go to Exercise:
10

Identify the prepositional phrase. Write it on the line.

14. The waitress is working in the front room.

11

_____

Rewrite the sentence fragments below to make complete sentences.

15. Rainy and stormy last night.

12

_____

16. Sheila's lunch break one hour.

13

_____

Change the punctuation in the following sentence to make two simple sentences.

17. I bought a new refrigerator, it was hard to find one that matched my stove.

14

_____

_____

Underline the dangling phrase in the following sentence.

18. Working carefully, the job was finished without any problems.

15

Underline any words that can be eliminated in this sentence.

19. Together, all combined our efforts together to made the project a success.

16

4   Pre-test

Place the commas where they are needed.

20. I need to go to the airport on Monday June 25.

21. The cafe owner served cheese crackers fruit and raw vegetables for the grand opening.

Underline the words that need to be capitalized in the following sentence.

22. My boss, mr. sardone, is vice president of hoffman insurance company.

Provide correct end punctuation for the following sentences.

23. Hurry, we will miss the train _____

24. No, I will not attend the meeting _____

25. Did you arrive on time for work _____

Exercise 1: Simple Sentences

> A **simple sentence** contains a simple subject and a simple predicate. It expresses a complete thought. The **simple subject** tells who or what the sentence is about. The **simple predicate** tells what the subject is or does.
>
> The fearless dog chased the frightened cat.
> **The simple subject is** <u>dog</u>. **The simple predicate is** <u>chased</u>.

Read each sentence below. Write the simple subject and simple predicate.

1. The factory needs better lighting.

    The simple subject is: _____   *The simple predicate is:* _____

2. The tired bus driver prepared for sleep.

    The simple subject is: _____   *The simple predicate is:* _____

3. The sound of falling trash cans startled the campers.

    The simple subject is: _____   *The simple predicate is:* _____

4. Joan wants to buy a new coat.

    The simple subject is: _____   *The simple predicate is:* _____

Write a simple sentence on each line. Use the subject and predicate given. The first one is done for you.

5. *subject:* Marta   *predicate:* received   <u>Marta received a raise.</u>

6. *subject:* Judy   *predicate:* helped

    _____

7. *subject:* friends   *predicate:* invited

    _____

8. *subject:* tornado   *predicate:* damaged

    _____

Directions: Choose the one best answer to each item. Circle the number of the correct answer.

Items 9 through 14 refer to the following paragraph.

(1) A buzzing sound disturbed the quiet night. (2) Hundreds of cicadas emerging from the soil! (3) These large insects take 17 years to develop. (4) They feed on the juices from tree roots. (5) Instinctively, the cicadas to the nearest trees to mate and lay eggs. (6) Adult cicadas live only a few weeks.

9. Sentence 1: **A buzzing sound disturbed the quiet night.**

    Why is this a simple sentence?

    (1) It shows sudden movement.
    (2) It tells about the night.
    (3) It asks a question.
    (4) It has a simple subject and a simple predicate.
    (5) It does not have a predicate.

10. Sentence 2: **Hundreds of cicadas emerging from the soil!**

    Why is this not a sentence?

    (1) It does not have a complete subject.
    (2) It has a complete predicate.
    (3) It is not a complete thought.
    (4) It is a complete thought.
    (5) It does not have a period at the end.

11. Sentence 3: **These large insects take 17 years to develop.**

    What is the simple subject of this sentence?

    (1) *These*
    (2) *large*
    (3) *insects*
    (4) *take*
    (5) *develop*

12. Sentence 4: **They feed on the juices from tree roots.**

    What is the simple predicate of this sentence?

    (1) *They*
    (2) *tree*
    (3) *roots*
    (4) *feed*
    (5) *from*

13. Sentence 5: **Instinctively, the cicadas to the nearest trees to mate and lay eggs.**

    What can be changed to make this a complete sentence?

    (1) Add a subject.
    (2) Add a verb.
    (3) Substitute a word for *Instinctively*.
    (4) Add two subjects.
    (5) No change is necessary.

14. Sentence 6: **Adult cicadas live only a few weeks.**

    What is the simple subject of this sentence?

    (1) *Adult*
    (2) *only*
    (3) *cicadas*
    (4) *weeks*
    (5) It has no subject.

7

Exercise 2: Interrogative Sentences

> An **interrogative sentence** asks a question. It contains a subject and a predicate. The predicate of an interrogative sentence comes before the subject. All interrogative sentences end with a question mark.
>
> Are you going to school tomorrow?
> **The subject is <u>you</u>. The predicate is <u>are going</u>.**

Read each interrogative sentence. Write the subject and predicate.

1. Is Tom listening for the baby?

   The subject is: _____   The predicate is: _____

2. Does he receive overtime pay?

   The subject is: _____   The predicate is: _____

3. Is your family taking a vacation this year?

   The subject is: _____   The predicate is: _____

4. When did Jamal buy the car?

   The subject is: _____   The predicate is: _____

Use the subject and predicate given to write an interrogative sentence on each line.

5. *subject:* chef   *predicate:* is preparing

   _____

6. *subject:* dog   *predicate:* does growl

   _____

7. *subject:* driver   *predicate:* has stopped

   _____

8. *subject:* artist   *predicate:* did complete

   _____

9. *subject:* flood   *predicate:* has damaged

   _____

Directions: Choose the one best answer to each item. Circle the number of the correct answer.

Items 10 through 15 refer to the following paragraph.

(1) What causes leaves to change color and fall from trees? (2) Why does the number of daylight hours vary throughout the year. (3) Thousands of years ago, ancient people wondered about these questions. (4) Each autumn they observed changes in their environment. (5) Do you know what ancient people thought about these changes? (6) They thought that the Earth was dying!

10. Sentence 1: **What causes leaves to change color and fall from trees?**

    Why is this an interrogative sentence?

    (1) It has a subject.
    (2) It makes a statement.
    (3) It lacks a predicate.
    (4) It asks a question.
    (5) It provides information about a predicate.

11. Sentence 2: **Why does the number of daylight hours vary throughout the year.**

    What correction should be made to this sentence?

    (1) Change *does* to *do*.
    (2) Place a question mark at the end of the sentence.
    (3) Insert a comma after *number*.
    (4) Change *number* to *numbers*.
    (5) No correction is necessary.

12. Sentence 3: **Thousands of years ago, ancient people wondered about these questions.**

    Why is this not an interrogative sentence?

    (1) It makes a statement.
    (2) It has no predicate.
    (3) The subject comes before the predicate.
    (4) It asks a question.
    (5) It lacks a subject.

13. Sentence 4: **Each autumn they observed changes in their environment.**

    How could this sentence be written as an interrogative sentence?

    (1) *They observed changes in their environment each autumn?*
    (2) *In their environment each autumn, they observed changes?*
    (3) *Did they observe changes in their environment each autumn?*
    (4) *Each autumn they observed changes in their environment?*
    (5) It cannot be written as an interrogative sentence.

14. Sentence 5: **Do you know what ancient people thought about these changes?**

    What is the simple subject of this interrogative sentence?

    (1) *people*
    (2) *do know*
    (3) *thought*
    (4) *changes*
    (5) *you*

15. Sentence 6: **They thought that the Earth was dying!**

    Why is this sentence not interrogative?

    (1) It contains two predicates.
    (2) It lacks a subject.
    (3) It asks a question.
    (4) It does not give a command.
    (5) It does not ask a question.

Exercise 3: Inverted Sentences

> In an **inverted sentence**, all or part of the verb precedes the subject. Interrogative sentences are usually inverted sentences.
>
> Where is the band playing today?
> **The simple subject is <u>band</u>. The verb is <u>is playing</u>.**
>
> Here are the latest reports.
> **The simple subject is <u>reports</u>. The verb is <u>are</u>.**

Read each inverted sentence. Underline the subject. Circle the verb.

1. Here *is* the <u>list</u> of participants in the charity auction.
2. *Is* <u>Josh</u> *making* dinner tonight?
3. There *are* the <u>books</u> for the library.
4. *Are* <u>you</u> *thinking* about taking that computer course?
5. When *will* <u>you</u> *punch* in your time card?

Write an inverted sentence containing the subject and verb given.

6. *subject:* Paula   *verb:* is coming

_____

7. *subject:* newspapers   *verb:* are

_____

8. *subject:* cashier   *verb:* is

_____

9. *subject:* traffic light   *verb:* is turning

_____

10. *subject:* trains   *verb:* are running

_____

Directions: Choose the one best answer to each item. Circle the number of the correct answer.

Items 11 through 16 refer to the following paragraph.

(1) Suddenly, there is no electricity at Walter's workshop. (2) Now he must find his way around in total darkness. (3) Where is the door to the office? (4) He does not know where he left his tool box. (5) Will he find his flashlight in his tool box? (6) At that moment, Walter finds his tool box. (7) Suddenly, the lights flicker back on!

11. Sentence 1: **Suddenly, there is no electricity at Walter's workshop.**

    Why is this an inverted sentence?

    (1) It lacks a subject.
    (2) It contains two verbs.
    (3) The verb appears before the subject.
    (4) It lacks a verb.
    (5) The subject comes before the verb.

12. Sentence 2: **Now he must find his way around in total darkness.**

    Why is this not an inverted sentence?

    (1) It lacks a subject.
    (2) It contains two verbs.
    (3) The verb appears before the subject.
    (4) It lacks a verb.
    (5) The subject comes before the verb.

13. Sentence 3: **Where is the door to the office?**

    What is the subject of this sentence?

    (1) *is*
    (2) *Where*
    (3) *office*
    (4) *to*
    (5) *door*

14. Sentence 4: **He does not know where he left his tool box.**

    How might this sentence be expressed as an inverted sentence?

    (1) *His tool box is not there.*
    (2) *He knows where his tool box is?*
    (3) *Where did he leave his tool box?*
    (4) *Walter knows the tool box is there.*
    (5) *The tool box is there.*

15. Sentence 5: **Will he find his flashlight in the tool box?**

    What is the simple subject of this sentence?

    (1) *flashlight*
    (2) *tool box*
    (3) *he*
    (4) *will find*
    (5) *box*

16. Sentence 7: **Suddenly, the lights flicker back on!**

    What are the subject and verb in this sentence?

    (1) *Suddenly* and *lights*
    (2) *Suddenly* and *flicker*
    (3) *back* and *on*
    (4) *lights* and *flicker*
    (5) *lights* and *on*

Imperative Sentences

> An **imperative sentence** gives a command. The subject is understood to be *you*. If the sentence shows strong emotion, it can end with an exclamation point.
>
> Give me the tickets.
> **The simple subject is understood to be <u>you</u>. The simple predicate is <u>give</u>.**
>
> Watch out for the car!
> **The simple subject is understood to be <u>you</u>. The simple predicate is <u>watch</u>.**
> **It ends with an <u>exclamation point</u> because it shows strong emotion.**

Write the subject and predicate. Choose the type of end punctuation.
The first one is done for you.

1. Close the file drawer when you are finished

   subject: _you (understood)_   predicate: _close_   punctuation: _a period_

2. Look for the blue sign

   subject: _____   predicate: _____   punctuation: _____

3. Take an umbrella to school

   subject: _____   predicate: _____   punctuation: _____

4. Send the letter now

   subject: _____   predicate: _____   punctuation: _____

Write an imperative sentence using the predicate and end punctuation.

5. *predicate:* deliver   *punctuation mark:* exclamation point

   _____

6. *predicate:* send   *punctuation mark:* period

   _____

7. *predicate:* stand   *punctuation mark:* exclamation point

   _____

8. *predicate:* leave   *punctuation mark:* exclamation point

   _____

Directions: Choose the one best answer to each item. Circle the number of the correct answer.

Items 9 through 14 refer to the following paragraph.

(1) The sign posted on the door gave the machinists safety tips for working around machinery. (2) *Wear your eye goggles.* (3) *Clean up your work area.* (4) *Remain silent while operating the equipment.* (5) Do you know what important statement was missing from this list? (6) Enjoy your day!

9. Sentence 1: **The sign posted on the door gave the machinists safety tips for working around machinery.**

   Why is this <u>not</u> an imperative sentence?

   (1) It asks a question.
   (2) It gives a command.
   (3) It makes a statement.
   (4) It lacks a verb.
   (5) The subject is understood to be you.

10. Sentence 2: ***Wear your eye goggles.***

    What is the subject of this imperative sentence?

    (1) *Wear*
    (2) *you* (understood)
    (3) *your*
    (4) *eye*
    (5) *goggles*

11. Sentence 3: ***Clean up your work area.***

    Why is this an imperative sentence?

    (1) It is a command.
    (2) It has a complete subject.
    (3) It is a request.
    (4) It is a statement.
    (5) all of the above

12. Sentence 4: ***Remain silent while operating the equipment.***

    What is the predicate of this imperative sentence?

    (1) *equipment*
    (2) *operating*
    (3) *while*
    (4) *silent*
    (5) *remain*

13. Sentence 5: **Do you know what important statement was missing from this list?**

    Why is this <u>not</u> an imperative sentence?

    (1) The subject is understood to be you.
    (2) It asks a question.
    (3) It gives a command.
    (4) It tells a story.
    (5) It lacks a predicate.

14. Sentence 6: **Enjoy your day!**

    Why does this sentence end with an exclamation point?

    (1) It asks a question.
    (2) It makes a statement.
    (3) It shows strong emotion.
    (4) It tells a story.
    (5) It lacks a subject.

Exercise 5: Compound Sentences

> A **compound sentence** is made up of two or more simple sentences. The simple sentences are joined by a conjunction such as *and, but, or, so, yet,* or *nor.* A comma is placed before the conjunction.
>
> **Simple Sentence 1:** Flashing lights indicated a train was approaching.
> **Simple Sentence 2:** The drivers did not stop.
> **Compound Sentence:** Flashing lights indicated a train was approaching, but the drivers did not stop.

Underline the simple sentences. Circle the conjunction that connects them.

1. We will go to the mall, or Carla will not receive an anniversary present.

2. It was too noisy for us there, so we moved to another apartment.

3. Mia loved the movie, but Zack found it quite boring.

4. I have the report, and I will read it tomorrow.

Combine each set of simple sentences to form a compound sentence.

5. The computer was not working properly. We called a technician to repair it.

   _____

6. I sent out invitations to the surprise party. Mel ordered food for the event.

   _____

7. We left early for the meeting. We were delayed by heavy traffic.

   _____

8. You can take the bus to school. You can walk to school to get some exercise.

   _____

9. The postal worker sorted the mail. She put it into the mailboxes.

   _____

Directions: Choose the one best answer to each item. Circle the number of the correct answer.

Items 10 through 14 refer to the following paragraph.

(1) Members of the Town Garden Club prepared for the annual plant, tree, and seed sale. (2) Evan placed price tags on the items. (3) Rita arranged the seed packets in alphabetical order. (4) Maria spent hours arranging the floral displays yet she never complained. (5) Peter watered, weeded, and fed the plants. (6) He enjoyed this job. (7) Ted designed posters advertising the sale. (8) Ann hung the signs all over town. (9) The day of the sale finally arrived and club members were convinced it would be a great success.

10. Sentence 1: **Members of the Town Garden Club prepared for the annual plant, tree, and seed sale.**

    Why is this not a compound sentence?

    (1) It has two conjunctions.
    (2) It does not contain two simple sentences.
    (3) It has no subject.
    (4) It has two commas.
    (5) It does not have a predicate.

11. Sentences 2 and 3: **Evan placed price tags on the items. Rita arranged the seed packets in alphabetical order.**

    How can you rewrite the underlined words to make a compound sentence?

    (1) *items, nor Rita*
    (2) *items, or Rita*
    (3) *items, and Rita*
    (4) *items and Rita*
    (5) A compound sentence cannot be made.

12. Sentence 4: **Maria spent hours arranging the floral displays yet she never complained.**

    What correction should be made to this sentence?

    (1) Place a comma before *yet*.
    (2) Place a comma before and after *yet*.
    (3) Place a comma after *hours* and after *displays*.
    (4) Place a comma after *hours* and after *yet*.
    (5) No correction is necessary.

13. Sentences 7 and 8: **Ted designed posters advertising the sale. Ann hung the signs all over town.**

    What is the best conjunction you can use to combine these sentences?

    (1) *but*
    (2) *yet*
    (3) *and*
    (4) *nor*
    (5) No conjunction can combine these sentences.

14. Sentence 9: **The day of the sale finally arrived and club members were convinced it would be a great success.**

    What correction should be made to this sentence?

    (1) Replace *and* with *so*.
    (2) Insert a comma after *and*.
    (3) Replace *arrived* with *arrives*.
    (4) Insert a comma after *arrived*.
    (5) No correction is necessary.

Exercise 6: Complex Sentences

> A **complex sentence** contains a dependent clause and a simple sentence.
> A **dependent clause** is a group of words that cannot stand alone. A dependent clause usually begins with a subordinating conjunction such as: *after, although, as long as, because, unless, until, when,* or *whenever.*
>
> **Dependent Clause:** Whenever I drive on this road
> **Simple Sentence:** I love to look at the beautiful trees.
> **Complex Sentence:** Whenever I drive on this road, I love to look at the beautiful trees.
>
> Use a comma after a dependent clause when it is the first part of a complex sentence. Do not use a comma if the dependent clause follows the simple sentence.
>
> As long as Connie studies the manual, she will be able to use the computer.
> Tony did not drive a car until he was thirty.

Read each complex sentence. Underline the dependent clause.

1. Because she was constantly late for work, Alice was fired from her job.

2. Rico gets the hiccups whenever he eats spicy food.

3. Tim never considered mountain climbing until he met Rhea.

4. After the severe thunderstorm, a rainbow appeared over the school.

5. Although our new dog makes a lot of noise, we like her.

Write a simple sentence for each dependent clause to form a complex sentence.

6. As long as we are going to the market, _____

7. Whenever Alice shops at that store, _____

8. unless I get to bed early tonight. _____

Directions: Choose the one best answer to each item. Circle the number of the correct answer.

Items 9 through 14 refer to the following paragraph.

(1) When Melanie had given up hope, she heard her father's truck pull into the driveway. (2) She sprang toward the door. (3) In spite of the fact that it was past her bedtime. (4) After flinging the door open Melanie shrieked with delight. (5) Her father held a recently abandoned dog he found at the animal shelter. (6) Although the young Labrador was frightened by its new surroundings, it managed a friendly yelp. (7) Ever since she had been promised a new dog one month ago Melanie had waited for this moment.

9. Sentence 1: **When Melanie had given up hope, she heard her father's truck pull into the driveway.**

    Why is this a complex sentence?

    (1) It contains two simple sentences.
    (2) It contains two predicates.
    (3) It contains a simple sentence and a dependent clause.
    (4) It contains two dependent clauses.
    (5) It contains two subjects.

10. Sentences 2 and 3: **She sprang toward the door. In spite of the fact that it was past her bedtime.**

    Which of the following is the best way to write the underlined portion of these sentences?

    (1) *the door in spite, of*
    (2) *the, door in spite of*
    (3) *the door in spite. Of*
    (4) *the door in spite of*
    (5) No correction is necessary.

11. Sentence 4: **After flinging the door open Melanie shrieked with delight.**

    What correction should be made to this sentence?

    (1) Insert a comma after *open*.
    (2) Insert a period after *door*.
    (3) Change *shrieked* to *shrieking*.
    (4) Change *after* to *before*.
    (5) No correction is necessary.

12. Sentence 5: **Her father held a recently abandoned dog he found at the animal shelter.**

    What correction should be made to this sentence?

    (1) Insert a comma after *recently*.
    (2) Change *abandoned* to *abandon*.
    (3) Change *animal shelter* to *Animal Shelter*.
    (4) Insert a comma after *abandoned*.
    (5) No correction is necessary.

13. Sentence 6: **Although the young Labrador was frightened by its new surroundings, it managed a friendly yelp.**

    What is the dependent clause in this complex sentence?

    (1) *it managed a friendly yelp.*
    (2) *by its new surroundings,*
    (3) *the young Labrador was frightened*
    (4) *a friendly yelp.*
    (5) *Although the young Labrador was frightened by its new surroundings,*

14. Sentence 7: **Ever since she had been promised a new dog one month ago Melanie had waited for this moment.**

    What correction should be made to this sentence?

    (1) Change *had* to *have*.
    (2) Insert a comma after *ago*.
    (3) Insert a period after *a new dog*.
    (4) Change *waited* to *waits*.
    (5) No correction is necessary.

Exercise 7: Parallel Structure

> Many sentences contain words and phrases that are connected by a conjunction. A sentence has **parallel structure** if the words or phrases are in the same form.
>
> **Structure not parallel:**
> The gardeners <u>weeded</u>, <u>watered</u>, and <u>were raking</u> the flower beds.
> **The underlined words are not in the same form. You can correct this sentence by changing <u>were raking</u> to <u>raked</u>.**
>
> **Correct parallel structure:**
> The gardeners <u>weeded</u>, <u>watered</u>, and <u>raked</u> the flower beds.

Underline the words or phrases with the same form in each sentence.

1. A true friend is loyal, trustworthy, and kind.

2. All day long, Eliza cooked meals, washed clothes, and cleaned floors.

3. Mark opened an account at the bank and then inquired about a car loan.

4. Tears of joy and shrieks of happiness greeted the bride and groom.

Look at the underlined word or phrase. Write the correct word or phrase on the line to give the sentence parallel structure.

5. As the fire alarm sounded, tenants of the building grabbed some belongings and <u>had run</u> toward the stairs. _____

6. Joel is seeking a girlfriend who participates in sports, <u>enjoying</u> country music, and likes to dance. _____

7. Meisha works out every day to reduce stress, <u>maintain</u> her weight, and to stay healthy. _____

8. Students attending the Art Institute learn how to paint with a variety of media and <u>sketching</u> landscapes. _____

9. The secretary copied, <u>had typed</u>, and stapled the weekly reports. _____

Directions: Choose the one best answer to each item. Circle the number of the correct answer.

Items 10 through 15 refer to the following paragraph.

(1) The new driver slowly, cautiously, and nervously maneuvered the vehicle down the street. (2) He forced himself to think about his actions and focus on the road. (3) Suddenly, a ball rolled into the street and had bounced toward his car. (4) He remembered and reflected on his driving instructor's words of caution. (5) He checks the rearview mirror and applied pressure to his brakes. (6) As the instructor had predicted, a young child darted into the street and picked up the ball.

10. Sentence 1: **The new driver slowly, cautiously, and nervously maneuvered the vehicle down the street.**

    What parallel words or phrases does this sentence contain?

    (1) *driver, vehicle, street*
    (2) *slowly, cautiously, nervously*
    (3) *new, the, down*
    (4) *cautiously, maneuvered, down*
    (5) *driver, maneuvered, street*

11. Sentence 2: **He forced himself to think about his actions and focus on the road.**

    What change would improve this sentence?

    (1) Change *think* to *thought*.
    (2) Insert a comma after *actions*.
    (3) Change *forced* to *forces*.
    (4) Insert *to* after *and*.
    (5) No correction is necessary.

12. Sentence 3: **Suddenly, a ball rolled into the street and had bounced toward his car.**

    Why is this sentence incorrect?

    (1) It does not contain words or phrases that are in the same form.
    (2) It contains too many words in the same form.
    (3) It does not contain a conjunction.
    (4) It has words in the same form.
    (5) It is correct.

13. Sentence 4: **He remembered and reflected on his driving instructor's words of caution.**

    Why is this sentence incorrect?

    (1) It does not contain the same words and phrases.
    (2) It does not have a subject.
    (3) It does not contain a conjunction.
    (4) all of the above
    (5) It is correct.

14. Sentence 5: **He checks the rearview mirror and applied pressure to his brakes.**

    What corrections should be made to this sentence?

    (1) Change *applied* to *applying*.
    (2) Change *mirror* to *mirrors*.
    (3) Change *checks* to *checked*.
    (4) Insert a comma after *and*.
    (5) No change is necessary.

15. Sentence 6: **As the instructor had predicted, a young child darted into the street and picked up the ball.**

    What similar words or phrases does this sentence contain?

    (1) *as* and *the*
    (2) *darted* and *picked*
    (3) *instructor* and *child*
    (4) *young, street,* and *ball*
    (5) *into* and *up*

Exercise 8: Misplaced Modifiers

> A **modifier** is a word or phrase that describes a word or group of words in a sentence. A modifier that is separated from the words it describes is called a **misplaced modifier**. Misplaced modifiers are incorrect and confuse or change the meaning of a sentence.
>
> Incorrect: The dog watched the letter carrier <u>barking</u>.
> In this sentence, <u>barking</u> seems to modify <u>letter carrier</u>.
> Correct: The <u>barking</u> dog watched the letter carrier.
>
> Incorrect: Virginia found the manual reaching high on the shelf.
> In this sentence, <u>reaching high on the shelf</u> seems to modify <u>manual</u>.
> Correct: <u>Reaching high on the shelf</u>, Virginia found the manual.

Circle the misplaced modifier in each sentence.

1. Destroyed by fire, Angela viewed her parent's home.

2. Rashid began to operate the machine looking carefully at the manual.

3. The books were returned by Lenny damaged in the shipping.

4. I often rent science-fiction movies to watch on Saturday nights from the video store.

Rewrite each sentence so that the misplaced modifier is closer to the word it describes.

5. The tenants complained to the housing committee who have no heat.

    _____

6. Marta placed the files in the new cabinet wanting to be helpful.

    _____

7. On my vacation I visited three European countries last month.

    _____

8. The shirt was a gift that I am wearing.

    _____

Directions: Choose the one best answer to each item. Circle the number of the correct answer.

Items 9 through 14 refer to the following paragraph.

(1) Everyone attended the sales meeting from my department. (2) We waited for the president of our company to present the safety award anxiously. (3) During the past year, our department was the safest always. (4) We were sure that our department was going to be the winner. (5) As the president stepped up to the microphone, all eyes focused on her and the huge plaque she was about to present.
(6) Now the plaque hangs on the wall in our department which is six feet tall.

9. Sentence 1: **Everyone attended the sales meeting from my department.**

   What correction should be made to this sentence?

   (1) Place *Everyone* after *meeting*.
   (2) Place a comma after *meeting*.
   (3) Place *from my department* after *Everyone*.
   (4) Place *attended the sales meeting* before *Everyone*.
   (5) No correction is necessary.

10. Sentence 2: **We waited for the president of our company to present the safety award anxiously.**

    What modifier is misplaced in this sentence?

    (1) *president*
    (2) *company*
    (3) *award*
    (4) *anxiously*
    (5) none of the above

11. Sentence 3: **During the past year, our department was the safest always.**

    What correction should be made to this sentence?

    (1) Place *department* after *always*.
    (2) Place *always* after *department*.
    (3) Place *always* after *was*.
    (4) all of the above
    (5) No correction is necessary.

12. Sentence 4: **We were sure that our department was going to be the winner.**

    What modifier is misplaced in this sentence?

    (1) *sure*
    (2) *department*
    (3) *winner*
    (4) all of the above
    (5) There is no misplaced modifier.

13. Sentence 5: **As the president stepped up to the microphone, <u>all eyes focused on her</u> and the huge plaque she was about to present.**

    How should the underlined phrase be corrected?

    (1) *all focused eyes were on her*
    (2) *all focused eyes were on the plaque*
    (3) *all eyes focused on the plaque*
    (4) *all eyes on her focused*
    (5) The phrase does not need to be corrected.

14. Sentence 6: **Now the plaque hangs on the wall in our department which is six feet tall.**

    What should *six feet tall* refer to in this sentence?

    (1) *the department*
    (2) *the president*
    (3) *the plaque*
    (4) *the microphone*
    (5) all of the above

Exercise 9: Subject-Verb Agreement

> Subjects and verbs must agree by matching in number. A singular subject must have a singular verb. A plural subject must have a plural verb.
>
> **Incorrect subject-verb agreement:**
> Every Tuesday, the doctors orders lunch from the coffee shop.
> The subject of this sentence is doctors. Doctors is a plural noun. The verb, orders, is singular. The verb should be order. The sentence lacks subject-verb agreement.
>
> **Correct subject-verb agreement:**
> Every Tuesday, the doctors order lunch from the coffee shop.

If the subject and verb agree, write *yes* on the line. If they do not agree, write *no*.

1. A notice is sent to the employees about the office move. _____

2. Many teachers have summer jobs unrelated to education. _____

3. Tenants from our building often meets in the laundry room. _____

4. Some politicians from my state attends the meeting each year. _____

5. The timid child cries every time it thunders. _____

Underline the form of the verb in parentheses that agrees with the subject.

6. Shoppers at the mall (scurry, scurries) to find a parking space.

7. A refund check from the electric company (is, are) coming today.

8. Millions of dollars worth of merchandise (was, were) destroyed.

9. Each book (has, have) a cover with the author's name on it.

10. We (know, knows) what is going to happen next.

11. He will let us (discover, discovers) the truth all on our own.

12. How many books (do, does) you have?

Directions: Choose the one best answer to each item. Circle the number of the correct answer.

Items 13 through 18 refer to the following paragraph.

(1) Thousands of people flocks to the beaches every summer. (2) The cool ocean air are a welcome relief from the city heat. (3) Some vacationers never sets foot on the sand. (4) Gazing at the ocean from the boardwalk are their preference. (5) Young children especially love swimming in the refreshing surf. (6) A vacation at the beach offers something for every member of the family!

13. Sentence 1: **Thousands of people flocks to the beaches every summer.**

    What correction should be made to this sentence?

    (1) Change *thousands* to *thousand*.
    (2) Change *flocks* to *flock*.
    (3) Change *summer* to *summers*.
    (4) Insert a comma after *people*.
    (5) No change is necessary.

14. Sentence 2: **The cool ocean air are a welcome relief from the city heat.**

    What change should be made to this sentence?

    (1) Change *air* to *airs*.
    (2) Change *are* to *is*.
    (3) Insert a comma after *air*.
    (4) Change *heat* to *heats*.
    (5) No change is necessary.

15. Sentence 3: **Some vacationers never sets foot on the sand.**

    Why is the word underlined in this sentence incorrect?

    (1) It does not agree with the subject.
    (2) It is singular.
    (3) It is plural.
    (4) The subject is singular and the verb is plural.
    (5) The underlined word is correct.

16. Sentence 4: **Gazing at the ocean from the boardwalk are their preference.**

    What correction should be made to this sentence?

    (1) Change *are* to *is*.
    (2) Insert a comma after *ocean*.
    (3) Change *boardwalk* to *boardwalks*.
    (4) Change *preference* to *preferences*.
    (5) No change is necessary.

17. Sentence 5: **Young children especially love swimming in the refreshing surf.**

    Why is the word underlined in this sentence incorrect?

    (1) *swimming* is a verb
    (2) *children* is singular
    (3) *love* is plural
    (4) *love* is singular
    (5) The underlined word is correct.

18. Sentence 6: **A vacation at the beach offers something for every member of the family!**

    What correction should be made to this sentence?

    (1) Insert a comma after *beach*.
    (2) Change *family* to *families*.
    (3) Change *beach* to *beaches*.
    (4) Change *offers* to *offer*.
    (5) No correction is necessary.

Exercise 10 Avoid Unnecessary Shifts in Tenses

> **Verb tense** indicates when an action occurred. All sentences in a paragraph should use the same tense.
>
> **Incorrect use of tenses:**
> Matt <u>rushed</u> toward his home. He <u>forgets</u> to turn off the stove before leaving that morning.
> **Past tense:** <u>rushed</u>   **Present tense:** <u>forgets</u>
>
> **Correct use of tenses:**
> Matt <u>rushed</u> toward his home. He <u>forgot</u> to turn off the stove before leaving that morning.

Read each passage. Underline the verbs. Write *yes* if the use of tenses is correct or *no* if the use of tenses is not correct.

1. Ricki will start a new job tomorrow. She is looking forward to working at the State University. She will be working in the financial office. _____

2. Zack will be traveling to the West Coast next month. He will visit relatives in San Diego and Los Angeles. He would like to have seen Anaheim as well. _____

3. A long line of cars remained motionless. The bridge was up and keeps traffic from moving over the river. Eugene shut off his car and settled back for a nap. _____

Read each passage. Underline each verb that shifts tense incorrectly. Then, write the correct form of each underlined verb on the line.

4. The crowd of spectators anticipates a great game. Last year's national champions play this year's only undefeated team. The matchup promised to be a real battle.

   _____

5. The chef finishes preparing the meal. Hours earlier, he created an incredible dessert. Suddenly, lots of hot sparks flew out from the oven.

   _____

Directions: Choose the one best answer to each item. Circle the number of the correct answer.

Items 6 through 11 refer to the following paragraph.

(1) Carlos placed the final box of items into his car. (2) He had been loading boxes into the vehicle since early morning. (3) He knows that moving would be a lot of work. (4) But, he has no idea that it would take this long! (5) After all, he was leaving a single room. (6) As he shut the trunk, Carlos vows not to allow his new apartment to get cluttered.

6. Sentence 1: **Carlos placed the final box of items into his car.**

    What is the verb in this sentence?

    (1) *box*
    (2) *items*
    (3) *placed*
    (4) *car*
    (5) *Carlos*

7. Sentence 2: **He had been loading boxes into the vehicle since early morning.**

    What time is indicated by the tense of the verb in this sentence?

    (1) present
    (2) past
    (3) future
    (4) either present or past
    (5) either present or future

8. Sentence 3: **He knows that moving would be a lot of work.**

    What correction should be made to the verb in this sentence?

    (1) Change *moving* to *moves*.
    (2) Change *would* to *will*.
    (3) Change *work* to *works*.
    (4) Change *knows* to *knew*.
    (5) No change is necessary.

9. Sentence 4: **But, he has no idea that it would take this long!**

    What correction should be made to this sentence?

    (1) Change *take* to *taken*.
    (2) Change *has* to *had*.
    (3) Change *idea* to *ideas*.
    (4) Change *long* to *longer*.
    (5) No change is necessary.

10. Sentence 5: **After all, he was leaving a single room.**

    What correction should be made to this sentence?

    (1) Change *room* to *rooms*.
    (2) Change *after all* to *someday*.
    (3) Change *leaving* to *leaves*.
    (4) Change *was* to *will*.
    (5) No correction is necessary.

11. Sentence 6: **As he shut the trunk, Carlos <u>vows</u> not to allow his new apartment to get cluttered.**

    Why is the underlined word incorrect?

    (1) It should be present tense.
    (2) It should be past tense.
    (3) It should be future tense.
    (4) It agrees with the subject.
    (5) It is not incorrect.

Exercise 11: Prepositional Phrases

> A **prepositional phrase** is a group of words that begins with a preposition and ends with a noun or pronoun. A prepositional phrase sometimes appears between the subject and verb of a sentence.
>
> **The verb must always agree with the subject, not the prepositional phrase.**
> The birds <u>in the tree</u> chirp merrily.
> |
>   prepositional phrase

Circle the prepositional phrase or phrases in each sentence.

1. The post office in our town is open on Sunday.

2. After a week in the new office, the workers started complaining about the air conditioning.

3. Adam was disturbed by the new rules.

4. The house for sale is owned by my uncle.

Write a sentence using each prepositional phrase.

5. inside the factory

6. after the thunderstorm

7. under the table

8. in the living room

9. at the sports arena

Directions: Choose the one best answer to each item. Circle the number of the correct answer.

Items 10 through 15 refer to the following paragraph.

(1) Preparations for the wedding went well. (2) The caterers from Oakville prepared all the food. (3) The florist created beautiful centerpieces for the tables. (4) Musicians from the band practiced a variety of the songs selected by the bride and groom. (5) The ceremony at Town Hall began promptly at noon. (6) All of the guests at the wedding had a memorable day.

10. Sentence 1: **Preparations for the wedding went well.**

    What is the prepositional phrase in this sentence?

    (1) *went well*
    (2) *wedding went*
    (3) *for the wedding*
    (4) *preparations for*
    (5) The sentence does not have a prepositional phrase.

11. Sentence 2: **The caterers from Oakville prepared all the food.**

    How many prepositional phrases are in this sentence?
    (1) one
    (2) two
    (3) three
    (4) four
    (5) none

12. Sentence 3: **The florist created beautiful centerpieces for the tables.**

    What does the prepositional phrase in this sentence describe?

    (1) *florist*
    (2) *beautiful*
    (3) *centerpieces*
    (4) *tables*
    (5) The sentence does not have a prepositional phrase.

13. Sentence 4: **Musicians from the band practiced a variety of the songs selected by the bride and groom.**

    How many prepositional phrases does this sentence contain?

    (1) one
    (2) two
    (3) three
    (4) four
    (5) none

14. Sentence 5: **The ceremony at Town Hall began promptly at noon.**

    What change should be made to this sentence?

    (1) Change *ceremony* to *ceremonies*.
    (2) Change *promptly* to *prompt*.
    (3) Insert a comma after *Hall*.
    (4) Change *began* to *begins*.
    (5) No change is necessary.

15. Sentence 6: **All <u>of the guests</u> at the wedding had a memorable day.**

    What does the underlined phrase in this sentence modify?

    (1) *day*
    (2) *guests*
    (3) *wedding*
    (4) *All*
    (5) The sentence does not have a prepositional phrase.

Exercise 12: Sentence Fragments Without Subject and Verb

> A **sentence fragment** is a group of words that does not express a complete thought.
>
> **Some sentence fragments lack a subject or a verb.**
> A meeting about employee benefits.
>
> **You can add a subject and verb to the fragment to create a simple sentence.**
> The committee held a meeting about employee benefits.

If the words form a sentence, write an *S* on the line. If they form a fragment, write an *F*.

1. Please wait at the door. _____

2. High above the fork lift. _____

3. After a delicious holiday dinner. _____

4. My ring is inside the box. _____

5. Along the winding highway. _____

Write a sentence on the line by adding a subject and verb to each sentence fragment.

6. of the finest quality

   _____

7. from the motor

   _____

8. at the new municipal center

   _____

9. because of bad weather

   _____

Directions: Choose the one best answer to each item. Circle the number of the correct answer.

Items 10 through 14 refer to the following paragraph.

(1) At the request of our mayor all businesses. (2) Will be closed next Monday. (3) Our community will celebrate the founding. (4) Of our town over 100 years ago. (5) Members of the centennial committee have prepared for this celebration. (6) For the past six months. (7) The day will open with a huge parade. (8) Down Main Street. (9) The celebration will end with a magnificent display of fireworks.

10. Sentence 1: **At the request of our mayor all businesses.**

    Why is this a sentence fragment?

    (1) It does not express a complete thought.
    (2) It lacks a subject.
    (3) It lacks a verb.
    (4) answers 1 and 3
    (5) answers 1, 2, and 3

11. Sentences 1 and 2: **At the request of our mayor all businesses. Will be closed next Monday.**

    What is the best way to combine these sentence fragments?

    (1) *At the request, of our mayor all businesses, will be closed next Monday.*
    (2) *At the request of our mayor all businesses will be closed, next Monday.*
    (3) *At the request of our mayor, all businesses will be closed next Monday.*
    (4) *At, the request of our mayor, all businesses will be closed, next Monday.*
    (5) No corrections are necessary.

12. Sentences 3 and 4: **Our community will celebrate the founding. Of our town over 100 years ago.**

    What is the best way to combine these groups of words?

    (1) Take out the period after *founding* and make *Of* lowercase.
    (2) Place a comma after *community* and take out the period after *founding*.
    (3) Place a comma after *celebrate* and take out the period after *founding*.
    (4) Place a comma after *town* and make *Of* lowercase.
    (5) none of the above

13. Sentences 5 and 6: **Members of the centennial committee have prepared for this <u>celebration. For</u> the past six months.**

    What changes should be made in the underlined words to combine them?

    (1) *celebration, for*
    (2) *celebration for*
    (3) *celebration for,*
    (4) *celebration, For*
    (5) These sentences cannot be combined.

14. Sentences 7 and 8: **The day will open with a huge parade. Down Main Street.**

    What is the best way to combine these groups of words?

    (1) *The day, will open with a huge parade down Main Street.*
    (2) *The day will open, with a huge parade down Main Street.*
    (3) *The day will open with a huge parade, down Main Street.*
    (4) *The day will open with a huge parade down Main Street.*
    (5) No correction is necessary.

Exercise 13: Sentence Fragments Without Verbs

> A **sentence fragment** with a subject but without a verb is a group of words that does not express a complete thought.
>
> **This sentence fragment contains a subject, but lacks a verb.**
> the <u>man</u> in the dark overcoat
> |
>   subject
>
> **You can add a verb to the fragment to create a simple sentence.**
> The man in the dark overcoat <u>won</u>.
> |
>   verb

Read each group of words. If they form a sentence, write an *S* on the line. If they form a sentence fragment, write an *F* on the line.

1. The paper in the copy machine. _____

2. A gifted artist in my neighborhood. _____

3. The author of this book signed my copy. _____

4. A guest speaker is coming today. _____

5. Before checking the rearview mirror, the careless driver. _____

Write a sentence on the line by adding to each sentence fragment.

6. Your package in the mail room

   _____

7. A statement from the bank

   _____

8. The work of the staff

   _____

9. While making photocopies, I

   _____

Directions: Choose the one best answer to each item. Circle the number of the correct answer.

Items 10 through 15 refer to the following paragraph.

(1) A large crowd of spectators.
(2) Watched the Memorial Day parade.
(3) Twenty bands from different municipalities.
(4) marched down Main Street. (5) Local organizations created floats for the occasion.
(6) Observers the float made by the owners of the flower shop in town. (7) Contained hundreds of roses and daisies. (8) In the shape of the American flag.

10. Sentence 1: **A large crowd of spectators.**

    Why is this group of words a sentence fragment?

    (1) It lacks a verb.
    (2) It does not form a complete thought.
    (3) It lacks a subject.
    (4) answers 1 and 2
    (5) answers 1, 2, and 3

11. Sentences 1 and 2: **A large crowd of spectators. Watched the Memorial Day parade.**

    What is the best way to rewrite these sentence fragments into a sentence?

    (1) *A large crowd of spectators, watched the Memorial Day parade.*
    (2) *A large crowd of spectators watched, the Memorial Day parade.*
    (3) *A large, crowd of spectators, watched the Memorial Day parade.*
    (4) *A large crowd of spectators watched the Memorial Day parade.*
    (5) *A large crowd, of spectators watched, the Memorial Day parade.*

12. Sentences 3 and 4: **Twenty bands from different municipalities. marched down Main Street.**

    What can be done to combine these sentence fragments?

    (1) Take out period after *municipalities*.
    (2) Replace the period after *municipalities* with a comma.
    (3) Capitalize *marched*.
    (4) Place a comma after *down*.
    (5) none of the above

13. Sentence 5: **Local organizations created floats for the occasion.**

    What is this group of words called?

    (1) a sentence fragment
    (2) a simple sentence
    (3) an interrogative sentence
    (4) a compound sentence
    (5) a complex sentence

14. Sentence 6: **Observers the float made by the owners of the flower shop in town.**

    What verb can you add to make this sentence fragment a sentence?

    (1) *to admire*
    (2) *admired*
    (3) *to see*
    (4) *seen*
    (5) *see*

15. Sentences 7 and 8: **Contained hundreds of roses and daisies. In the shape of the American flag.**

    Which of the two groups of words is a sentence fragment?

    (1) *Contained hundreds of roses and daisies.*
    (2) *In the shape of the American flag.*
    (3) *hundreds of roses and daisies*
    (4) Both are sentence fragments.
    (5) Both are simple sentences.

Exercise 14: Run-on Sentences

> A **run-on sentence** is usually two sentences written as a single sentence.
>
> **Two sentences form this run-on sentence.**
> Jon awoke at dawn, a barking dog had disturbed his sleep.
>
> **They should be written as two single sentences.**
> Jon awoke at dawn. A barking dog had disturbed his sleep.

Circle each single sentence in each run-on sentence.

1. Jill carefully opened the box she screamed when she saw a diamond ring.

2. Mitchell called me today he is coming for a visit next week.

3. Ira and Joan had a huge argument they broke their engagement.

4. Where are my keys, I left them on the kitchen table.

Rewrite each run-on sentence as two simple sentences.

5. Rita is eager to leave for vacation she is leaving tomorrow.

   _____

6. In the middle of the movie, Eva felt ill, she left the theater.

   _____

7. Bob was happy he worked hard, he got an A.

   _____

8. Sally and I were so excited, we found good jobs!

   _____

9. Give me the name of that book, I want to check it out at the library.

   _____

Directions: Choose the one best answer to each item. Circle the number of the correct answer.

Items 10 through 14 refer to the following paragraph.

(1) Danny nervously entered the bustling airport, it was a hub of activity because of the holiday. (2) Until today, he had never flown on an airplane. (3) Danny checked his watch, his flight was scheduled to leave in less than an hour. (4) He didn't want to miss his first flight. (5) After asking for directions, he scrambled down a long hallway, when he reached the gate, he discovered the flight was delayed.

10. Sentence 1: **Danny nervously entered the bustling airport, it was a hub of activity because of the holiday.**

    What is this group of words called?

    (1) a simple sentence
    (2) a sentence fragment
    (3) a run-on sentence
    (4) an interrogative sentence
    (5) a compound sentence

11. Sentence 2: **Until today, he had never flown on an airplane.**

    What correction should be made to this sentence?

    (1) Omit the comma.
    (2) Change the period to a question mark.
    (3) Insert a comma after *flown*.
    (4) Insert a period after *he*.
    (5) No correction is necessary.

12. Sentence 3: **Danny checked his watch, his flight was scheduled to leave in less than an hour.**

    What corrections should be made to this sentence?

    (1) Capitalize *his* and insert a comma after *scheduled*.
    (2) Change the period to an exclamation point.
    (3) Insert a comma after *flight*.
    (4) Change the comma to a period and capitalize *His*.
    (5) No change is necessary.

13. Sentence 4: **He didn't want to miss his first flight.**

    Why is this sentence not a run-on sentence?

    (1) It has a subject.
    (2) It has a predicate.
    (3) It doesn't have a subject and a verb.
    (4) It is one complete sentence.
    (5) It is a compound sentence

14. Sentence 5: **After asking for directions, he scrambled down a long hallway, when he reached the gate, he discovered the flight was delayed.**

    What correction should be made to this sentence?

    (1) Omit the comma after *directions* and capitalize *he*.
    (2) Change the comma after *hallway* to a period and capitalize *when*.
    (3) Change the comma after *gate* to a period and capitalize *he*.
    (4) Capitalize *when*.
    (5) No correction is necessary.

Exercise 15: Dangling Phrases

A **dangling phrase** is a group of words that is not placed correctly in a sentence. Sentences with dangling phrases are confusing.

After calling the company, her phone did not work.
Dangling phrase: After calling the company,
Dangling phrase: her phone did not work

The way the sentence above is written, it sounds as though the phone called the company. In order to make the sentence clear, you must rewrite one of the phrases.
After Carol called the phone company, her phone did not work.

Read each sentence. What do you need to know about each dangling phrase? Write *who?* or *what?* on the line. The first one is done for you.

1. Due to illness, will miss school today. _who?_

2. Holly quickly opened to the apartment. _____

3. Always punches out at the end of the day. _____

4. Were sent to all the neighbors. _____

5. After checking the car, said the service was free. _____

Correct each sentence by rewriting the dangling phrases. Write the sentence on the line. The first one is done for you.

6. While driving to Connecticut, the highway was crowded.

   While driving to Connecticut, we saw that the highway was crowded.

7. Soaked by the sudden rainstorm, the bus was a welcome sight.

   _____

8. After visiting the dentist, his teeth were clean.

   _____

Directions: Choose the one best answer to each item. Circle the number of the correct answer.

Items 9 through 13 refer to the following paragraph.

(1) Fly from New York to California every day. (2) Many people take a morning flight to California, so have a full day upon arrival. (3) Because of the time change, you can have breakfast in New York and again in California! (4) Flying is especially nice to California in the winter. (5) Can leave New York, with its winter snow, and arrive in warm, sunny California in only a few hours.

9. Sentence 1: **Fly from New York to California every day.**

   What is missing from this sentence?

   (1) the verb
   (2) the subject
   (3) a preposition
   (4) all of the above
   (5) The sentence is correct.

10. Sentence 2: **Many people take a morning flight to California, so have a full day upon arrival.**

    What correction should be made to this sentence?

    (1) Insert a comma after *morning*.
    (2) Insert *they* after *so*.
    (3) Insert *person* after *so*.
    (4) Insert *they* after *upon*.
    (5) No correction is necessary.

11. Sentence 3: **Because of the time change, you can have breakfast in New York and again in California!**

    What is the dangling phrase in this sentence?

    (1) *Because of the time change,*
    (2) *can have breakfast*
    (3) *again in California!*
    (4) all of the above
    (5) There is no dangling phrase in this sentence.

12. Sentence 4: **Flying is especially nice to California in the winter.**

    How should this sentence be rewritten?

    (1) *In the winter to California, flying is especially nice.*
    (2) *Flying is nice in the winter to California.*
    (3) *Flying is especially nice in the winter to California.*
    (4) *Flying to California is especially nice in the winter.*
    (5) No correction is necessary.

13. Sentence 5: **Can leave New York, with its winter snow, and arrive in warm, sunny California in only a few hours.**

    What is the dangling phrase in this sentence?

    (1) *with its winter snow,*
    (2) *Can leave New York*
    (3) *arrive in warm, sunny California*
    (4) *warm, sunny*
    (5) *California in only a few hours.*

Exercise 16: Avoid Wordiness

> Wordiness is the use of too many words in a sentence. You can avoid wordiness by omitting words that repeat the same ideas.
>
> The <u>woman</u> at the front desk <u>she</u> took the customer's order.
> **The word she should be omitted from this sentence. The reader understands that the woman at the front desk took the order.**
>
> <u>In my opinion</u>, I think the movie is enjoyable.
> **In my opinion is a useless phrase in this sentence.**

Read each sentence. Underline the word or words that should be omitted.

1. Due to the fact that because Jane was sick, the meeting was canceled.

2. The car that I sold yesterday it is in good condition.

3. My older sister she looks younger than me!

4. San Francisco is rainy and cold in December, as wet and chilly as you can imagine.

5. We gathered together around the table.

Omit any unnecessary words from the sentence. Write the new sentence on the line. The first one is done for you.

6. Ted purchased a jacket blue in color and heavy in weight.

   <u>Ted purchased a heavy, blue jacket.</u>

7. In many instances and often, Tina missed the train.

   _____

8. Although our mayor is young in age, he is a good leader.

   _____

9. The customers rushed into the opened store when the doors opened.

   _____

Directions: Choose the one best answer to each item. Circle the number of the correct answer.

Items 10 through 14 refer to the following paragraph.

(1) Rewiring the vacant, run-down, empty house on Oak Street was quite an experience for the new electrician. (2) Some of the other electricians at the shop they frightened the new man. (3) They told tales about occurrences that were strange in the house. (4) Some people believed that in the house there may have lived ghosts. (5) After a long day in duration, the electrician finished the work in the house and dashed out before it became dark.

10. Sentence 1: **Rewiring the vacant, run-down, empty house on Oak Street was quite an experience for the new electrician.**

    What can be omitted in this sentence?

    (1) *Rewiring*
    (2) *empty*
    (3) *Oak Street*
    (4) *experience*
    (5) *new*

11. Sentence 2: **Some of the other electricians at the shop they frightened the new man.**

    What word should be omitted from this sentence?

    (1) *electricians*
    (2) *shop*
    (3) *they*
    (4) *frightened*
    (5) Nothing can be omitted.

12. Sentence 3: They told <u>tales about occurrences that were strange</u> in the house.

    What is the best way to rewrite the underlined words in this sentence?

    (1) *that tales were strange*
    (2) *tales about strange occurrences*
    (3) *strange tales about the house occurrences*
    (4) *about occurrences that were strange tales*
    (5) No change is necessary.

13. Sentence 4: **Some people believed that <u>in the house there may have lived ghosts</u>.**

    What is the best way to rewrite the underlined words in this sentence?

    (1) *ghosts once lived in the house.*
    (2) *the house had ghosts who were once living in it.*
    (3) *ghosts were in the house to live in it.*
    (4) *house ghosts lived in the house.*
    (5) No change is necessary.

14. Sentence 5: **After a long day in duration, the electrician finished the work in the house and dashed out before it became dark.**

    What word or words make this sentence wordy?

    (1) *After a long day*
    (2) *finished the work*
    (3) *in duration*
    (4) *dashed out*
    (5) The sentence is not wordy.

Exercise 17: Commas

> **Commas** are used to separate parts of a date or address, as well as a series of items. They also set off sentence interrupters and introductory words or phrases.
>
> The wedding will be held on <u>Sunday, October 29</u>. ← Date
> The library is at <u>332 Grove Street, Wellesley, Massachusetts</u>. ← Address
> Sid placed cabbages, carrots, and potatoes on the kitchen counter. ← Series of items
> My boss, <u>Mr. Brown,</u> has the office next to mine. ← Sentence interrupter
> <u>Yes,</u> I will take the job. ← Introductory word
> <u>After Marta recovered</u>, she returned to work. ← Introductory phrase
>
> **Use a comma when a sentence begins with a dependent clause.**
> Because the tire was flat, Becky could not drive her car.
>
> **Use a comma when you join two complete thoughts with *and*, *but*, and *or*.**
> Jack has been with the company three years, and he has never been late.

Read each sentence. Insert a comma where needed.

1. This job offers good health benefits and the people are very friendly.

2. Tia's new address will be 6 Carefree Lane Jupiter Florida.

3. At three o'clock on Monday April 7 I will leave for Mexico.

4. Send the letter to Maximum Care Corporation 222 First Avenue Dallas Texas.

5. When Ahmed was ill Tanya did all of the household chores.

6. This postcard was sent from London England on Friday December 1.

Correct any sentences that have wrongly placed commas. Some sentences are correct.

7. Betty and Charlene work the day shift at the paper factory.

8. All the employees, are happy with the new contract.

9. Copy, and staple these papers before putting them in the boxes.

10. The new green, and white uniforms are easy to wash and iron.

Directions: Choose the one best answer to each item. Circle the number of the correct answer.

Items 11 through 15 refer to the following passage.

(1) The new hospital wing will open on Tuesday June 2. (2) All lab technicians medical assistants and custodians are to report to work promptly at 8 o'clock A.M. (3) Parking stickers will be issued for all employees the day before Monday, June 1. (4) Be sure to show your employee card driver's license, or any other form of identification to pick up your sticker. (5) The new wing is very large so if you cannot find your way around, please feel free to ask the security guard at the reception desk.

11. Sentence 1: **The new hospital wing will open on Tuesday June 2.**

    Where should the commas be placed in this sentence?

    (1) after *new*
    (2) after *hospital*
    (3) after *wing*
    (4) after *Tuesday*
    (5) No comma is necessary.

12. Sentence 2: **All lab technicians medical assistants and custodians are to report to work promptly at 8 o'clock A.M.**

    What correction should be made to this sentence?

    (1) Insert a comma after *technicians*.
    (2) Insert a comma after *assistants*.
    (3) Insert a comma after *custodians*.
    (4) both 1 and 2
    (5) No correction is necessary.

13. Sentence 3: **Parking stickers will be issued for all employees the day before Monday, June 1.**

    What correction should be made to this sentence?

    (1) Take out the comma after *Monday*.
    (2) Add a comma after *employees*.
    (3) Add a comma after *before*.
    (4) all of the above
    (5) No correction is necessary.

14. Sentence 4: **Be sure to show your employee card driver's license, or any other form of identification to pick up your sticker.**

    What correction should be made to this sentence?

    (1) Omit the comma after *license*.
    (2) Insert a comma after *card*.
    (3) Insert a comma after *identification*.
    (4) all of the above
    (5) No correction is necessary.

15. Sentence 5: **The new wing is very large so if you cannot find your way around, please feel free to ask the security guard at the reception desk.**

    Where should the comma be placed in this sentence?

    (1) after *large*
    (2) after *so*
    (3) after *free*
    (4) after *guard*
    (5) No changes are necessary.

Exercise 18: Capitalization

> The first word of every sentence and the pronoun *I* are always **capitalized**. Capitalize proper nouns such as names, places, events, days of the week, months, and words used as titles (only when the title is part of a proper noun).
>
> Most of my relatives will attend the party. ← Sentence
> I am looking forward to seeing them tonight. ← Pronoun *I*
> Diana will spend New Year's Eve visiting the Grand Canyon. ← Event
> Tuesday is the first day of spring. ← Day of week
> Susan is writing to Assemblyman Maynard about taxes. ← Title

Circle the words in each sentence that should be capitalized.

1. what time is your flight, sandy?

2. because my grandparents were born in poland, my family speaks polish at home.

3. i will spend the fourth of july in bermuda with leon.

4. last year julie moved from denver, colorado, to los angeles, california.

5. after my training, i will be working in atlanta, georgia.

6. during the month of august, bill can be found swimming in the atlantic ocean.

7. are mark and zack going to the real estate agent's open house?

8. without notice, rhea suddenly moved to belmont street.

9. i was shocked to discover my luggage was in paris, france!

10. all the employees of middletown printing company attended a party honoring mrs. dunston, the president.

11. evan was born on the first wednesday in october.

12. i will meet with tim on the second and fourth sundays in january.

13. the fair will be held in countryside park on saturday, october 29.

14. my neighbor, mayor sutton, performed a marriage ceremony on tuesday, february 14.

Directions: Choose the <u>one best answer</u> to each item. Circle the number of the correct answer.

<u>Items 15 through 20</u> refer to the following paragraph.

(1) For the past several years, the Finest packaging Company has closed for two weeks during the month of january. (2) This Year was no exception. (3) My manager and his family went to a ski lodge in vail, Colorado. (4) The office Administrator, ms. Myers, vacationed in sunny spain. (5) She is taking an extra week and will not return to the United States until february. (6) As for myself, like many other employees of the company, I spent the two weeks in january simply relaxing!

15. Sentence 1: **For the past several years, the Finest packaging Company has closed for two weeks during the month of january.**

    What correction should be made to this sentence?

    (1) Capitalize *years.*
    (2) Capitalize *packaging.*
    (3) Capitalize *january.*
    (4) both 2 and 3
    (5) The sentence is correct.

16. Sentence 2: **This Year was no exception.**

    What correction should be made to this sentence?

    (1) Omit the capital from *This.*
    (2) Omit the capital from *Year.*
    (3) Capitalize *exception.*
    (4) all of the above
    (5) No correction is necessary.

17. Sentence 3: **My manager and his family went to a ski lodge in vail, Colorado.**

    How many capitalization errors are there in this sentence?

    (1) one
    (2) two
    (3) three
    (4) four
    (5) none

18. Sentence 4: **The office Administrator, ms. Myers, vacationed in sunny spain.**

    What correction should be made to this sentence?

    (1) Omit the capital from *Administrator.*
    (2) Capitalize *ms.*
    (3) Capitalize *spain.*
    (4) all of the above
    (5) No correction is necessary.

19. Sentence 5: **She is taking an extra week and will not return to the United States until february.**

    What corrrection should be made to this sentence?

    (1) Omit capital from *States.*
    (2) Capitalize *week.*
    (3) Capitalize *february.*
    (4) all of the above
    (5) No correction is necessary.

20. Sentence 6: **As for myself, like many other employees of the company, I spent the two weeks in january simply relaxing!**

    How many words that are not capitalized need to be corrected in this sentence?

    (1) one
    (2) two
    (3) three
    (4) four
    (5) none

Exercise 19: End Punctuation

> A sentence must end with a punctuation mark.
>
> **Simple sentences end with a period.**
> The computer training classes begin next week.
>
> **Interrogative sentences end with a question mark.**
> Where do you live, Sharon?
>
> **Commands end with a period.**
> Get the milk from the refrigerator.
>
> **A sentence that shows strong emotion ends with an exclamation point.**
> Sandy has lost her wallet!

Read each sentence. Put a period, question mark, or exclamation point on the line.

1. Give me your car keys _____

2. Did you get enough sleep last night _____

3. The stove is on fire _____

4. Ted has been working here two years longer than Pete _____

5. Are you going to the meeting with Tina _____

Create the type of sentence described. Write your sentence with the correct end punctuation. An example is done for you.

6. Simple sentence

   We gave Gina a surprise bridal shower yesterday.

   _____

7. Interrogative sentence

   _____

8. Command

   _____

Directions: Choose the one best answer to each item. Circle the number of the correct answer.

Items 9 through 13 refer to the following paragraph.

(1) Have you ever spent a day with a toddler. (2) If so, you probably know what my day is like as a child care worker. (3) Child care workers need to keep up with a youngster's steady stream of energy and constant motion (4) It's a difficult job because you have to be alert every minute of the day? (5) The only break I usually get is during nap time!

9. Sentence 1: **Have you ever spent a day with a toddler.**

    What correction should be made to this sentence?

    (1) Insert a period after *day*.
    (2) Change the period to a question mark.
    (3) Change the period to an exclamation point.
    (4) Insert a comma after *you*.
    (5) No correction is necessary.

10. Sentence 2: **If so, you probably know what my day is like as a child care worker.**

    What correction should be made to this sentence?

    (1) Add a question mark after *worker*.
    (2) Add an exclamation point after *worker*.
    (3) Insert a comma after *energy*.
    (4) Insert a comma after *steady*.
    (5) The sentence is correct.

11. Sentence 3: **Child care workers need to keep up with a youngster's steady stream of energy and constant motion**

    How can this sentence be corrected?

    (1) Add a question mark at the end of the sentence.
    (2) Add a period at the end of the sentence.
    (3) Add an exclamation point at the end of the sentence.
    (4) Add a comma at the end of the sentence.
    (5) No correction is necessary.

12. Sentence 4: **It's a difficult job because you have to be alert every minute of the day?**

    What correction should be made to this sentence?

    (1) Change the question mark to an exclamation point.
    (2) Change the question mark to a comma.
    (3) Change the question mark to a period.
    (4) all of the above
    (5) No correction is necessary.

13. Sentence 5: **The only break I usually get is during nap time!**

    What change can be made to this sentence?

    (1) Insert a period after *break*.
    (2) Insert a question mark after *get*.
    (3) Change the exclamation point to a period.
    (4) Change the exclamation point to a question mark.
    (5) No correction is necessary.

Post Test

The following post test will help you determine where you need further practice in *Sentences*. Take the test in one sitting, answering every question. If you need more practice, return to the Exercises listed.

For additional review, go to Exercise:

Read the sentence below. Write the simple subject and simple predicate.

1. The frightened ostrich runs on hoof-like feet. [1]

   The simple subject is: _____   The simple predicate is: _____

Identify the following sentence as interrogative or imperative.

2. May I please borrow a sheet of paper? _____ [2]

Read the inverted sentence. Write the simple subject and verb.

3. Is the pharmacist filling Mikio's prescription? [3]

   Simple subject: _____   Verb: _____

Identify the understood subject in the sentence below.

4. Help your little sister walk across the street. [4]

   The understood subject is: _____

Join the following simple sentences to create a compound sentence.

5. Emperor penguins live in the Antarctic. [5]

   They survive sub-zero temperatures and freezing winds.

   _____

Which word in the following sentence joins two compound sentences?

6. Did you finish your science in class, or are you waiting for a tutorial? _____ [5]

Read the complex sentence below. Underline the dependent clause.

7. After the storm passed, volunteers repaired the damaged library. [6]

Correct the following sentence by changing the words or phrases to the same form. Write the new sentence on the lines.

8. To get in shape, I plan to stretch every morning, jog three times a week, and swimming on weekends. [7]

   _____

   _____